THE GENTLE AUTHOR'S CRIES OF LONDON

PEACE

the Gentle Author's CRIES OF LONDON

Spitalfields Life
Books

First published in 2015 by Spitalfields Life Books Ltd

© The Gentle Author

A CIP record for this book is available from the
British Library

978-0-9576569-8-7

A Spitalfields Life Book
Edited by The Gentle Author

Designed by David Pearson
Albion Buildings, Back Hill
Clerkenwell
London EC1R 5HT
www.typeasimage.com
@typeasimage

Published by Spitalfields Life Books Ltd
16 Victoria Cottages
Spitalfields
London E1 5AJ
www.spitalfieldslife.com
@thegentleauthor

Printed by Legatoria Editoriale Giovanni Olivotto Spa
Viale Dell'Industria 2
36100 Vicenza
Italy

Typeset in Miller (designed by Matthew Carter), Brunel &
Chiswick (designed by Paul Barnes)

Frontispiece
A street musician mimics the notes of common English birds by
means of a folded bit of tin which he holds between his teeth but,
in order to engage the attention of the credulous, he pretends to
draw his tones from rubbing two tobacco pipes together—drawn
by John Thomas Smith

Contents

Winchester Street, London Wall, drawn in May 1801.

INTRODUCTION

ILLUSTRATED WITH ETCHINGS BY JOHN THOMAS SMITH

IN THE MIDST OF LIFE you wake in the dark city of your dreaming. It was the bellman that woke you before dawn, crying wearily, 'Past three o'clock and a cold frosty morning,' before he stumbled away with lamp in hand and mutt in tow through the gloomy passage. In the distance of your half-waking, you hear 'Buy a dish a flounders' and 'Give you good morrow, my masters,' before you fall back into your slumber again.

At sunrise, the streets are already teeming. 'Fine Seville oranges, fine lemons, fine,' cries the orange woman. 'Buy any milk below,' cries the dairy maid, as a chorus of hawkers fills the streets calling like birds chattering in trees—'Wood to cleave'—'Fine hot cakes'—'Hot eel pies'—'Buy any garlic'—'Good sausages'—'New sprats new'—'Buy any buttons'—'Featherbeds to dry'—'Clove water, stomach water'—'Ripe walnuts ripe' and 'Quick winkles, quick, quick, quick.' You close the casement, bar the shutter, pull the curtain and wrap the pillow round your ears to resist the clamour.

When you wake again, it is daybreak and there is a tumult of Criers beneath the window—'Have you any work for a tinker?'—'Buy a fine singing bird'—'Sixpence a pound, fair cherries'—'Any baking pears?'—'Old shoes for new brooms'—'Twelve pence a peck, oysters'—'Lights for the cats, liver for the dogs'—'Buy an almanac'—'Hot spiced gingerbread'—'Two bunches a penny, primroses'—'Buy a barrel of samphire'—'Pity the poor prisoners' and 'What is't ye lack?'

You rise and walk out into the street. Now they cry 'Banana, banana, banana!'—'Lamb biriani, chicken biriani, one pound'—'Standard, standard'—'Come on ladies, come on ladies, one pound fish, one pound fish.' There are fake DVD hawkers, gipsies with lucky heather, *Big Issue* sellers, whisperers offering 'a smoke,' nitrous oxide pedlars, evangelists, street dancers, ticket touts, curry touts, charity canvassers, street dancers and human statues. They are offering free samples of wood-fired pizza, frappuccinos and frozen yoghurt.

Five hundred years of Cries of London passed in the street while you were dozing.

❋

Beneath Leadenhall Market lie the ruins of the Roman forum and basilica as evidence that London has existed for over two millennia as a marketplace, revealing that the culture of street trading is as old as the city itself. Through centuries, the dispossessed and those with no other income were always able to cry wares in the streets of London. By turning their presence into performance with their Cries they claimed those streets as their theatre, winning the lasting affections of generations of Londoners and embodying the soul of the city in the popular imagination. Thus, through time, the cultural legacy of the Cries became integral to the distinctive identity of London. This book traces the historical evolution of images of Criers, comprising an illustrated survey of street life in the capital over four centuries.

Undertaking interviews with stallholders in Spitalfields, Brick Lane, Columbia Road and other East End markets in recent years led me to consider the culture of street trading. While this phenomenon might appear transitory and fleeting, I discovered a venerable tradition in the Cries of London. Yet even this genre of popular illustrated prints, which began in the seventeenth century, was itself preceded by verse such as *London Lackpenny* attributed to the fifteenth century poet John Lydgate that drew upon an earlier oral culture of hawkers' Cries. From medieval times, the great number of Cries in London became recognised by travellers throughout Europe as indicative of the infinite variety of life in the British capital.

Given the former ubiquity of the Cries of London, the sophistication of many of the images, their significance as social history, and their existence as almost the only portraits of working people in London through four centuries, it astonishes me that there have been so few books upon this subject. This volume sets out towards redressing this imbalance, including several sets of Cries that are almost unknown to the wider public.

I take my cue from Samuel Pepys who pasted three sets of Cries into his albums of London & Westminster in a chronological sequence spanning a century, thereby permitting an assessment of the evolution of the style of the prints as well as social change in the capital in his era. In this volume, I have reproduced these and supplemented them with another dozen series published in the following centuries, which trace the development of the Cries right into our own time.

The innumerable sets of Cries of London produced, with different publishers and artists copying and republishing each others' work, make a comprehensive survey of this subject impossible. Instead, I have collated a personal selection of those that delight me, those that speak most eloquently of the life of the street and those created by artists who demonstrated an affinity with the Criers.

Through the narrow urban thoroughfares and byways, hawkers announced their wares by calling out a repeated phrase that grew familiar to their customers, who learned to recognise the Cries of those from whom they bought regularly. By nature of repetition, these Cries acquired a musical quality as hawkers improvised upon the sounds of the words, evolving phrases into songs. Commonly, Cries also became unintelligible to those who did not already know what was being sold. Sometimes the outcome was melodic and lyrical, drawing the appreciation of bystanders, and at other times discordant and raucous as hawkers strained their voices to be heard across the longest distance.

Over time, certain Cries became widely adopted, and it is in written accounts and songbooks that we find the earliest records, predating the visual images of Criers featured in this book. These print collections of pictures of Criers also became known as 'Cries' and although the oldest set in London dates from around 1600, there are those from Paris which predate these by a century. Characteristically, the Cries represented peripatetic street traders or pedlars, yet other street characters were also included from the start. At first, the Cries were supplemented by the bellman and the town-crier but then preachers, beggars, musicians and performers were added as the notion of the Cries of London became expanded by artists and print sellers seeking greater novelty through elaborating upon the original premise.

Among the Criers, there were distinctions to be drawn and closely guarded by the traders themselves, especially between some who chose to see themselves as respectable businessmen and women—such as bakers supplying fresh produce to frequent customers on a round—and those itinerants passing through, who were customarily judged to be no better than vagabonds.

Among these itinerants, there were categories of hawkers and pedlars. There were those who came from outside the city, rising before dawn to bring fresh fruits and vegetables such as strawberries or cucumbers that they had grown or gathered, and those who touted newly-killed small game including rabbits and wildfowl. There were simplers who specialised in foraging and dealing herbs and medicinal plants. There were costermongers and fishwives who bought produce daily from the London wholesale markets and sold it across the city. There were artisans selling household items manufactured by their own hand or by their families, offering products such as doormats, hat boxes or kitchen implements. There were dealers offering products such as crockery or brooms in exchange for secondhand goods, clothes or boots. There were those offering services, such as chair menders, sweeps, knife grinders or tinkers. There were those distributing printed publications—chapbooks, ballads, almanacs, playbills and newspapers.

Then there were buskers and other street performers, professionals on tour and local talents, charity collectors and beggars, including war veterans, the physically handicapped and the mentally ill, alongside magicians, street gamblers, card sharks, confidence tricksters, pickpockets, pimps, prostitutes and muggers.

Before the age of traffic, the streets of London offered a common public space for all manner of activity, trading, commerce, sport, entertainment and political rallies. Yet this arena of possibility, which is the primary source of the capital's cultural vitality, has also invited the consistent attention of those who seek policing and social control upon the premise of protecting citizens from each other, guarding against crime and preventing civil unrest. It suits the interest of those who would rule the city that, in London, street traders have always been perceived as equivocal characters with an identity barely distinguished from vagrants. Thus the suspicion that their itinerant nature facilitated thieving and illicit dealing, or that women might be selling their bodies as well as their legitimate wares has never been dispelled.

Like the internet, the notion of the street as a space where people may communicate and do business freely can be profoundly threatening to some. It is a tension institutionalised in this country through the issuing of licences to traders, criminalising those denied such official endorsement, while on the continent of Europe the right to sell in the street is automatically granted to every citizen. Depending upon your point of view, the itinerants are those who bring life to the city through their occupation of its streets or they are outcasts who have no place in a developed modern urban environment.

When I interviewed Tony Purser on his last afternoon after fifty-two years selling flowers outside Fenchurch Street Station in the City of London, he admitted to me that as a boy he assisted his father Alfie, and, before licences were granted in 1962, they were both regularly arrested. Their stock was confis-cated, they were charged three shillings and spent the night in the cells at Bishopsgate Police Station, before going back to trade again next day.

I was told that in Brick Lane, until recently, it was possible for casual traders to buy five pounds' worth of parking tickets from a machine as a day's licence, but when this was withdrawn, those who had always sold their possessions on the pavement on Sunday mornings found themselves on the wrong side of the regulations. Prior to the opening of a shopping mall of sea containers for international brands on the former Bishopsgate Goods Yard, I witnessed fly-pitchers in their eighties and nineties turfed off the pavement by dubious enforcement officers who pilfered the best of their wares.

Yet in this part of London, the heartland of markets and street trading, there is a long-held understanding that those who have no job, no shop or stall have always been able to sell things in the street and make a living for themselves. I know several people who spend their days searching dustbins in the East End and make a living by selling their finds on Brick Lane each Sunday, and students who sell off their clothes and textbooks each week to buy groceries. I met a man who sold baked potatoes outside the Tower of London and opened a restaurant that became a chain. I know a spoon carver who sat on the pavement carving spoons until he saved the deposit to rent a shop. Last year, I interviewed a recently-divorced electrician who had his tools taken away and became a Directions Man, making an income by standing outside Liverpool Street Station and showing visitors the way.

Street trading proposes an interpretation of the ancient myth of London as a city paved with gold that is not without truth. Many large British corporate retailers including Tesco, started by Jack Cohen in 1919, and Marks & Spencer, started by Michael Marks in 1884, owe their origin to single stalls in markets —emphasising the value of street trading to wider economic development. Meanwhile, Oxford Street

*NORTH EAST VIEW OF AN OLD HOUSE LATELY STANDING IN SWEEDON'S PASSAGE,
GRUB STREET, DRAWN IN JULY 1791.*

SOUTH EAST VIEW OF THE OLD HOUSE LATELY STANDING IN SWEEDON'S PASSAGE, GRUB STREET, DRAWN IN JULY 1791.

HOUSES LATELY STANDING ON THE WEST CORNER OF
CHANCERY LANE, FLEET STREET, DRAWN IN AUGUST 1789.

HOUSES ON THE SOUTH SIDE OF LEADENHALL STREET,
DRAWN IN JULY 1796.

Association seeks to rid the pavement of souvenir sellers between the large department stores, and the current trend towards the privatisation of public spaces sees the increasing introduction of bylaws restricting trading solely to those legitimised by the property owners.

The story of Tony Hawkins, a licensed pedlar who was arrested eighty-seven times for legally selling caramelised peanuts in the West End of London, concludes this book. He told me that on each occasion, he was beaten up and had his stock confiscated even though he had the right to trade under the Pedlars Act of 1871. I include his account both as a snapshot of the contemporary situation for hawkers and also as testimony to the ongoing struggle of street traders, who have been consistently marginalised by the authorities in London through the centuries yet managed to thrive and endure regardless, through heroic tenacity and strength of will.

In the twentieth century, the Cries of London found their way onto cigarette cards, chocolate boxes, biscuit tins, tea towels, silk scarves, dinner services and, famously, tins of Yardley talcum powder from 1913 onwards, becoming divorced from the reality they once represented as time went by, copied and re-copied by different artists.

Yet the sentimentally cheerful tones applied by hand to prints, that were contrived to appeal to the casual purchaser, chime with the resilience required by traders selling in the street. And it is our respect for their spirit and resourcefulness which may account for the long lasting popularity of these poignant images of the self-respecting poor who turned their trades into performances. Even now, it is impossible to hear the cries of market traders and newspaper sellers without succumbing to their spell, as the last reverberations of a great cacophonous symphony echoing across time and through the streets of London.

Surely none can resist the romance of the Cries of London and the raffish appeal of the liberty of vagabondage, of those who had no indenture or task master, and who travelled wide throughout the city, witnessing the spectacle of its streets, speaking with a wide variety of customers, and seeing life. In the densely-populated neighbourhoods, it was the

VIEW OF PART OF DUKE STREET, WEST SMITHFIELD, DRAWN IN JULY 1807.

OLD HOUSES LATELY STANDING AT THE SOUTH CORNER OF HOSIER LANE, SMITHFIELD, DRAWN IN APRIL 1795.

itinerants' cries that marked the times of day and announced the changing seasons of the year. Before the motorcar, their calls were a constant of street life in London. Before advertising, their songs were the jingles that announced the arrival of the latest, freshest produce or appealing gimcrack. Before radio, television and internet, they were the harbingers of news, and gossip, and novelty ballads. These itinerants had nothing but they had possession of the city.

I write these words just a stone's throw from Brick Lane, where Lionel Begleiter grew up in a first floor flat on the corner of Princelet Street in the nineteen-thirties. Although I do not know on which corner he lived, there is one building with a small window where I can imagine Lionel, as a little boy, leaning out to wonder at the Cries in Brick Lane. As 'Lionel Bart' in 1960, he wrote *Oliver!*, the only enduring theatrical dramatisation of Charles Dickens' work, integrating both music hall and folk song into the stage musical with spectacular success. His setting of Cries of London, as 'Who will buy this wonderful morning?' remains the most evocative musical manifestation in the collective consciousness.

I leave you with the words of most celebrated Crier in our own century—Muhammad Shahid Nazir, the 'One Pound Fish Man' of Queen's Market in Upton Park—as an example of the acclaim and status that Criers can win in London through their wit, ingenuity and performance skill. Nazir became an internet sensation with fourteen million views on Youtube, won a recording contract and is now a pop star in Pakistan.

'Come on ladies, come on ladies
One pound fish
Have-a, have-a look
One pound fish
Very, very good, very, very cheap
One pound fish
Six for five pound
One pound each'

The Cries of London have taught me the essential truth of London street traders down through the centuries, and it is one that still holds today—they do not need your sympathy, they only want your respect, and your money.

Houses on the South side of London Wall, drawn in March 1808.

CHAPTER ONE

SAMUEL PEPY'S CRIES ANTIENT & MODERNE

THE EARLIEST COLLECTION of Cries of London is that which once belonged to Samuel Pepys. Driven by his acquisitive nature and infinite curiosity about life, he amassed more than ten thousand engravings and eighteen hundred printed ballads, including several sets of Cries of London. Alongside those Cries published in his own day, Pepys included those of a generation before, which are among the oldest surviving examples—a significant juxtaposition suggesting he recognised the value of these prints as documents of social history.

In his final years, Pepys organised his print collection into albums within his library with the assistance of Paul Lorrain and two others. He subsequently bequeathed the collection to Magdalene College, Cambridge, where he had studied as an undergraduate and where his legacy is preserved to this day. These three thousand volumes that Pepys had bound, catalogued according to his own system and stored in cases manufactured to his design in the workshops at Chatham dockyard, can be seen as a natural complement to his personal writing—gathering together essential cultural texts and images of the physical world, just as his journal recorded salient details of his experience of daily life.

In two large albums entitled *London & Westminster*, Pepys collected his topographical, historical and architectural prints of these locations, including a section labelled 'Cryes consisting of Several Setts thereof, Antient & Moderne: with the differ Stiles us'd therein by the Cryers.' In these folios were pasted three series of Cries of London on successive pages, placing them as an integral part of the identity of the city as much as the lofty monuments of brick and stone.

Arranged in chronological sequence of their publication, these three sets illustrate the evolution of the form of the Cries during the seventeenth century, from a single sheet to a chapbook to a series of individual prints. The earliest set in Pepys' collection, believed to date from the beginning of the seventeenth century, is described thus: 'A very antient Sett thereof, in Wood, with the Words then used by the Cryers.'

Twenty-four alternating male and female Criers inhabit gothic niches in four storeys of arcades. Obeying the conventional attitudes of formal portraiture in which men turn to the right and women to the left, they display wares as symbols to indicate their identities, like medieval saints parading upon an altarpiece. Suggesting a procession through time, they are introduced by the town-crier at daybreak and interrupted by the bellman and the watchman, just as the various Criers each had their own place within the rhythm of the passing hours.

This is followed on the next page by a set of thirty-two engravings believed to date from around 1640, described by Pepys as 'A later Sett, in Wood—with the Words also then in use.' By comparison with the woodcuts representing stereotypical figures of Criers, these have more self-possession—though close examination reveals that the same models recur, posing in a variety of guises as different street vendors. Yet in spite of these enacted tableaux, there exists a convincing presence of distinct personalities among these Criers—glancing around in circumspection or meeting our gaze with implacable stoicism.

These two anonymous sets from the early and mid-seventeenth century, pasted across double page spreads, are succeeded by pages containing a series of individual prints by Marcellus Laroon published in 1687, illustrating the Cries that were 'moderne' for Pepys to the degree he could caption eighteen of them with the name of Criers that were known to him.

Thus, turning the large folio pages of *London & Westminster* invites comparison—permitting Samuel Pepys to contrast those 'antient' prints from his parents' generation with those of his youth and adulthood, contemplating the hawkers that populated the streets of the city before he was born, distinguishing the differences in their clothing and wares, and wondering at how London had changed in his time.

The Cryer.   *Kitchin=Stuff.*   *The Fidler's Goodw...*

Bread & Meat for y̆   *My Rope of Onyons*   *Ends of Gold or S...*
poor Prisoners.   *white St Thom? Onyons.*

Waintfleet=Oysters.   Chimney=Sweep.   Rosemary & Bays.

ott Pudding-Pyes hott.   Buy a Matt for a Bed.   Hott Codlings.

Bread & Meat for ÿ   My Rope of Onyons   Ends of Gold or S
poor Prisoners.   white St Thom! Onyons.

Maids hang-out Your Lights.   Fine Sevil Oranges   Buy a Hair=Li
                                 Fine Lemons.   or a Jack=Line

Maids in Your Smocks   Buy a fine Toast.ng Fork.   Old Shooes or B
Look to Your Locks.   Come buy my P

Hott Pudding-Pyes hott.   Buy a Matt for a Bed.   Hott Codlings.

White Radish White   Buy my marking Stones.   Who buys my fine Sau=
young Lettice.   =sidge.

my fine wash Balls.   Buy Ink & Pens ye best,   Come Glasses, Glasses,
                        Seconds ye least.   fine Glasses.

Haue you any worke for a Tinker work for a Tinker.

Old showes or Bootes will yu buy some Broome.

Buy a hone or a whetstone or a marking stone.

A Tanker bearer

Codlinges hot hot Codlinges.

Radishes or lettis tow bunches a peny.

Macarell new Macakrell.

Bandestringes or hankercher buttons

Haue you any Chaires to mend.

Matt for a Doore Bed buy a matt.

Chimney Sweepe.

Worke for Cooper worke for Cooper.

Br a Coche or a gelding.

New wall fleete Oysters.

Buy my Hartichokes Mistris.

Mussels Lilly Mussels white

Maribones Maides maribones.

Buy a steele or a Tinder Box

Ells er yeards by yeard er Ells.

Lanthorne and a whole Candell light, hange out your ligats heare

fine Oranges fine Lemons

I ha ripe Couccumber, ripe Couccumber

White Vnions whitt St. Thomas Vnions

I haue ripe straw:buryes ripe Strawburyes

I haue Screenes if you Desier to keepe yr Butey from yr fire

Some broken Breade and meate for yr poore prisnors for the lords sake pitey the poore

Small Cole a penny a peake

Buy a Brosh or a table Booke

Buy my dish of great Smelts

What kichin stuffe haue you Maides

I haue fresh Cheese and Creame I haue fresh

New flounders new

CHAPTER TWO

MARCELLUS LAROON'S CRYES
DRAWNE AFTER THE LIFE

WHEN THE GREAT FIRE of 1666 destroyed shops and markets, an unprecedented horde of hawkers flocked to the city from across the country to supply the needs of Londoners. Among the first Cries to be credited to an individual artist, Marcellus Laroon's *Cryes of the City of London Drawne after the Life* were on a more ambitious scale than had been attempted, permitting sophisticated use of composition and greater detail in costume.

Hawkers were portrayed not merely as representative types but each with a distinctive personality, revealed through their movement, their attitudes, their postures, their gestures and their clothing, according to the wares they sold. Perhaps influenced by Bonnart's *Cries de Paris* and Carraci's drawings in Bologna, Laroon's Cries possessed more vigour and individuality than those that had gone before, reflecting the dynamic renewal of London at the end of the seventeenth century.

Such was their success, Laroon's original set of forty designs commissioned by the entrepreneurial bookseller Pierce Tempest in 1687 was quickly expanded to seventy-four and continued to be reprinted from the same plates until 1821.

Living in Bow Street, Covent Garden, from 1680 until his death in 1702, Laroon sketched those he came to know in his years of residence there. Expanding the range of subjects beyond hawkers and watchmen, he included street performers, a prostitute, tricksters, dubious clergymen and other hustlers. For the first time, the swagger and the performance that is essential to success as a street trader was manifest.

The details of Marcellus Laroon's life are scarce and conjectural. A Frenchman born in the Hague, Laroon was reputedly an acquaintance of Rembrandt as a young man. He may have become drawing master to King William III when he came to London, but was primarily employed as a costume painter in the portrait studio of Sir Godfrey Kneller. According to Bainbrigg Buckeridge, author of the earliest history of English painting entitled *An Essay Towards An English School of Painters*, Laroon was 'an exact Draftsman but chiefly famous for Drapery, wherein he exceeded most of his contemporaries.'

Fragmentary evidence connects Samuel Pepys and Marcellus Laroon. The 'Harwich' portrait of Pepys—so-called because it shows the channel port in the background—is believed to be by Laroon and to date from around 1685, while Godfrey Kneller painted Pepys' portrait in 1689, which perhaps contains drapery by Laroon. Certainly, Pepys acquired drawings by Laroon of the Lord Mayor's Show and other subjects which he collected into his albums alongside engravings of Laroon's Cries.

Unlike the highly-formalised portraits upon which he was employed by Kneller, Laroon's *Cryes of the City of London Drawne after the Life* demonstrate an inventive variety of pose and spontaneity of composition. Each subject is permitted individual attention with close observation to the detail of their clothing as an integral expression of their identity. Portrayed with an unsentimental balance of stylisation and realism, all Laroon's figures are presented with grace and poise, even if they are wretched.

Since Laroon's designs were ink drawings produced under commission to Pierce Tempest, he achieved little personal reward or success from the subsequent exploitation of his creations, earning his day-to-day living by painting the drapery for Kneller's aristocratic portraits and then dying of consumption at the age of forty-nine.

Yet, through widening the range of subjects of the Cries to include all social classes as well as preachers, beggars and performers, Marcellus Laroon left us a shrewd and exuberant vision of the variety of London street life in his day.

Six pence a pound fair Cherryes.

A Bed Matt or a Door Matt.

A Brass Pott or an Iron Pott to mend.

Colly Molly Puffe.

Maids buy a Mapp.

New River Water.

Fine Writeing Inke.

Remember the Poor Prisoners.

Any Work for Iohn Cooper?

The Famous Dutch Woman.

Old Chaires to mend.

Buy my Dish of great Eeles.

Buy a fine Singing Bird.

The Squire of Alsatia.

Knives, Combs or Inkhornes.

The Merry Milk Maid.

Old Cloaks, Suits or Coats.

Notes on several plates

Six Pence a Pound Fair Cherryes—Itinerant traders such as this costermonger were only permitted to buy produce at Covent Garden Market after the restaurants and hotels had picked their choice of the crop.

Colly Molly Puffe hawked fruit pies, cakes, gingerbread and jam tarts but was famous for his puff pastries, and enjoyed his swiftest business at public events such as parades, coronations and executions.

New River Water—In 1613, Sir Hugh Middleton completed a thirty-eight mile canal bringing water from Hertfordshire and, from 1626 onwards, water porters made daily rounds from conduits and pumps, charging customers a penny or tuppence per gallon delivered to their door.

Remember the Poor Prisoners—Parishes often appointed former prisoners with baskets and collecting boxes to beg food and money for current inmates, who had to pay for their own cells and bedding while incarcerated.

The Famous Dutch Woman—Mrs Cornelius Saftry was first described performing by Robert Hooke on 30th August 1677, 'Saw the Dutch woeman in Bartholomew Fair, very strange,' and according to *The Post Boy*, she was still there in 1701, offering the additional attraction of 'An Italian Scaramouch who Dances on the Rope with two Children and a Dog in a Wheel Barrow, and a duck on his Head.'

The Squire of Alsatia—Bully Dawson was a notorious gambler, card-sharp, swindler and libertine, described by James Granger in his *Biographical Dictionary of England* as, 'one of the gamesters of Whitefriars, which was notorious for these pests of society, who were generally dressed to the extremity of the mode.' Of low birth, Dawson affected aristocratic dress to seduce wealthy women and lure gambling partners of quality. Operating from the ancient sanctuary of Whitefriars, he died at forty-three in the Lock of Southwark.

Knives, Combs or Inkhornes—Pedlars were the most numerous of itinerants, selling novelties primarily to women. Many pedlars were Scottish and in 1683, suffering the most suspicion of nefarious activity, they petitioned Charles II for just treatment.

The Merry Milk Maid—This is believed to be a portrait of Kate Smith. On May Day, it was the custom for milk maids to dance before the houses of their customers, with churns upon their heads decorated with silver plate, ribbons and flowers.

The Old Clothes Man—Oliver Cromwell re-admitted Jews to Britain in 1656 and Marcellus Laroon's drawing of a dealer in old cloaks, suits and coats is the earliest representation of a trade that was pursued by Jewish people through subsequent centuries, traditionally indicated by the wearing of several hats.

CHAPTER THREE

PAUL SANDBY'S CRIES DONE FROM LIFE

OBSERVE THE YOUNG WOMAN displaying her travelling peep show containing the views of Paul Sandby's *Cries of London Done From Life*, while in the background the artist is seen carrying packets of his prints back to his house in Carnaby Market, Soho, where he sold them directly to customers from the door—becoming a hawker in his own right.

Recognised today along with his brother Thomas as a landscape watercolourist, Paul Sandby's hundred or so sketches of street traders—of which only a dozen were issued as engravings—proved to be a misdirection in his career, yet they are distinguished by a greater realism than had previously been brought to the subject of the Cries.

Both Paul and Thomas trained in military drawing at the Tower of London. Paul then assisted in the surveying of the Highlands of Scotland after the defeat of the Jacobite Rebellion. He began to paint landscapes in his spare time, before going to live with Thomas in Windsor Great Park where his brother had been appointed Deputy Ranger. Over a decade there, Paul established himself as a consummate landscape painter with his views of Windsor, winning the admiration of Thomas Gainsborough.

In 1760, Paul Sandby moved to London and set up house in Soho upon his marriage, and his series of Cries may be understood as his response to the city after years in Windsor. He saw with the eyes of an outsider to London, and perhaps his military training encouraged a certain objectivity and lack of sentiment regarding hawkers. In Scotland, he mapped the land as part of the subjugation of the rebels and, in London, he mapped the underclass of street traders.

These are the first Cries in which the traders are portrayed as dirty. As well as undertaking individual portraits, Sandby placed each of his Criers in a dramatic relationship to the world. Far from merely picturesque, these hawkers confront us in ways we might seek to avoid, especially the seller of switches for the infliction of domestic punishment who raises his arm as if he might lash out at us.

Thus Sandby granted power and independent life to his subjects. Rather than simply amusing curiosities, these hawkers are the first to demand our respect. While in life we might have taken detours or done almost anything to evade them, Sandby's Cries propose a more complex and troubling political relationship than had been described formerly.

Unsurprisingly, Sandby found that the public did not warm to this portrayal of the urban social landscape with the same enthusiasm which they responded to his rural landscapes. Beyond the set of twelve engravings, none of the other hundred sketches were ever turned into prints.

In 1760, Sandby displayed his rural landscapes as part of the Society of Artists which became the Royal Academy when it was incorporated by George III in 1765, with Sandby chosen to be one of the twenty-eight founder members in 1768. For the rest of his career, Sandby sublimated his figures to landscapes, existing as polite adornments to add scale to the majesty of scenes which established his reputation and provided a livelihood—but he never did better figure drawings than in his characterful and raggedy *Cries of London Done From Life*.

Lights for the cats, liver for the dogs.

26

My pretty little Gimy Tarters for a hapenny a stick.

Do you want a good flint or steel?

Pots and pans!

Chapter Four

Francis Wheatley's
London Cries

Francis Wheatley exhibited his series of thirteen oil paintings of *London Cries* at the Royal Academy over three years beginning in 1792. Two years earlier, the forty-three-year-old painter had been elected as an Associate to the Academy by sixteen votes to three in preference to Thomas Lawrence, the King's nominee, and—as a consequence—he scarcely secured any further commissions for portraits from the aristocracy. He lost his income entirely and, becoming an Academician, which should have been the crowning glory of his career, was its unravelling. Wheatley was declared insolvent in 1793 and struggled to make a living until his death in 1801 at fifty-four years old in King's Bench Walk prison, when the Royal Academy paid his funeral expenses.

In the midst of this turmoil, lacking aristocratic sitters, Wheatley created these images of street sellers which, although regarded in his lifetime as of little consequence beside his society portraits, are now the works upon which his reputation rests.

Born in 1746 and raised in Wild Court, Covent Garden, Wheatley was ideally qualified to portray these hawkers because he grew up amongst them and their cries, echoing in the streets around the market. The stone pillars of Covent Garden may be recognised in a couple of these pictures, all of which were located in the vicinity of the market.

However, these idealised images are far from social reportage, and you may notice a certain similarity between many of the women portrayed in them. It is believed his second wife, Clara Maria Leigh—a painter and exhibitor at the Royal Academy in her own right—was the model for these women. Look again, and you will also see variants of the same ginger and white terrier occurring in these paintings—this is understood to be Wheatley's dog. The languorous poise and artful drapery of Wheatley's figures suggest classical models, as if these hawkers were the urban equivalents of the swains and shepherdesses of the pastoral world. Influenced by Jean-Baptiste Greuze, Wheatley had painted agricultural workers at harvest and several of the Criers he depicted are those who came to the city to sell their produce.

Although too late to save his career, Wheatley was well served by his engravers who created the prints which brought recognition for his Cries. Luigi Schiavonetti, born in Bassano in 1765, engraved the first three plates, the Primrose Seller, the Milk Maids and the Orange Seller, with lush velvety stippled tones—a style that was maintained by the three subsequent engravers (Cardon, Vendramini and Gaugain), when Schiavonetti became too successful and expensive for such a modest project. Wheatley's Cries were sold at seven shillings and sixpence for a plain set and sixteen shillings coloured, and the fact that all thirteen were issued is itself a measure of their popularity.

It was an unlikely choice for Francis Wheatley to paint Cries of London at the time he was losing grip on his life—struggling under the pressure of increasing debt—since they cannot have been an obvious commercial proposition.

Yet I like to surmise that these fine images celebrate the qualities of the people that Wheatley—like Laroon before him—experienced first-hand in the streets and markets, growing up in Covent Garden, and chose to witness in this affectionate and subtly-political set of pictures, existing in pertinent contrast to the portraits of rich patrons who shunned him when he was in need.

Two Bunches a Penny, Primroses, Two Bunches a Penny!

Strawberrys, Scarlet Strawberrys.

Old Chairs to Mend.

Turnips & Carrots, ho !

Hot Spice Gingerbread, Smoaking Hot !

Fresh Gathered Peas, Young Hastings.

CHAPTER FIVE

WILLIAM MARSHALL CRAIG'S
ITINERANT TRADERS

As FRESH AS THE DAY they were hand-tinted in 1804, these plates from William Marshall Craig's *Itinerant Traders of London in their Ordinary Costume with Notices of Remarkable Places given in the Background* were bound into the back of Richard Phillips' *Modern London* and the vibrancy of their pristine hues suggests they have never been exposed to daylight in two centuries.

A portrait artist who exhibited regularly at the Royal Academy between 1788 and 1827, William Marshall Craig was appointed painter in watercolours to Queen Charlotte, and in this set of prints he dignifies his itinerant traders, allowing them self-possession even as they proffer their wares in eager expectation of a sale.

Despite their colourful representation with rosy cheeks and clothes of pantomime prettiness, in his drawings engraved onto thirty-one plates by Edward Edwards, Marshall Craig acknowledges the dignity of working people, admitting the vulnerability and occasional weariness of those who woke in the dawn to spend their days trudging the streets, crying their wares in all weathers.

Marshall Craig placed each of his itinerants within a picturesque view of London, thus giving extra value to the buyer by simultaneously celebrating the wonders of architectural development as well as the infinite variety of street traders. But there is a disparity between the modest humanity of the hawkers and the meticulously rendered monumentalism of the city. These characters are as out of place as those unreal figures in artists' impression of contemporary developments, included only to sell the latest scheme.

Even as the noble buildings, circuses and squares of Georgian London speak of the collective desire for social order, the presence of the hawkers manifests the playful anarchy of those who came singing down the street.

Hair Brooms.

Cats & Dogs Meat !

Dust O !

Chairs to Mend.

Buy a Bill of the Play.

Sweep Soot O !

Mackerel.

Hot Spiced Gingerbread.

Lavender.

Slippers.

NOTES ON THE PLATES

Excerpts from descriptions accompanying the plates in Richard Phillips' Modern London, 1804

HAIR BROOMS, HEARTH BROOMS, BRUSHES, SIEVES, BOWLS, CLOTHES HORSES AND ALMOST EVERY ARTICLE OF TURNERY—Some of these turners travel with a cart, but the greater number carry the shop on their shoulders, and find customers sufficient to afford them a decent subsistence, the profit on turnery being considerable and the consumption certain. (Shoreditch Church is a church of peculiar beauty. It has a portico in front, elevated upon a flight of steps and enclosed with an iron railing, which is disgraced by a plantation of poplar trees.)

CATS' & DOGS' MEAT, consisting of horse flesh, bullocks' livers and tripe cutting. The two former are sold by weight at twopence per pound and the latter tied up in bunches of one penny. Although this is the most disagreeable commodity cried for sale in London, the occupation seems to be engrossed by women. As soon as one of these purveyors arrives, she is surrounded by a crowd of animals, and were she not as severe as vigilant, could scarcely avoid the depredations of her hungry followers. (Bethlem Hospital stands on the south side of Moorfields. On each side of the iron gate is a figure, one of melancholy and the other of raging madness.)

DUST O!—Dust carts ply the streets through the morning in every part of the metropolis. Two men go with each cart, ringing a large bell and calling 'Dust O!' daily, they empty the dust bins of all the refuse that is thrown into them. The ashes are sold for manure, the cinders for fuel and the bones to the burning houses. (New Church in the Strand, contiguous to Somerset House and dividing the very street in two.)

CHAIRS TO MEND—Mending chairs is generally conducted by a family or a partnership. One carries the bundle of rush and collects old chairs, while the workman, seating himself in some corner on the pavement, exercises his trade. For small repairs they charge from fourpence to one shilling and for newly covering a chair from eighteen pence to half a crown. It is necessary to bargain prior to the delivery of the chairs or the chair mender will demand an exorbitant compensation for his time and labour. (Soho Square, a square enclosure with shrubbery at the centre, begun in the time of Charles II.)

BUY A BILL OF THE PLAY—The theatres are surrounded, as soon as they open, with the Criers of playbills. These are mostly women who also carry baskets of fruit. The titles of the play and entertainment, and the name and character of every performer, are found in the bills, which are printed at the expense of the theatre and sold by the hundred to the Criers, who retail them at one penny, unless fruit is bought, when they will present their customer a bill of the play gratis. (Drury Lane Theatre, part of the colonnade fronting to Russell Street, Covent Garden.)

SWEEP SOOT O!—A master sweep patrols for custom attended by two or three boys, the taller ones carrying the bag of soot, and directing the diminutive creature who, stripped perfectly naked, ascends and cleans the chimney. The hard condition of the sweep devolves upon the smallest and feeblest of the children apprenticed from the parish workhouse.

(Foundling Hospital, a handsome building in Guildford Street, stands at the upper end of a large piece of ground in which the children play in fine weather.)

MACKEREL—More plentiful than any other fish, mackerel affords a livelihood to sellers who cry them through the streets every day, not excepting Sunday. Mackerel boats being allowed by act of Parliament to dispose of their perishable cargo on Sunday morning, prior to the commencement of divine service. No other fish partake that privilege. (Billingsgate Market commences at three o'clock in the morning in summer and four in winter.)

HOT SPICED GINGERBREAD, Sold in cakes of one halfpenny each, very well made, well baked and kept extremely hot, is a very pleasing regale in cold and gloomy evenings. In the long light days of summer, this seller takes his stand near the portico of the Pantheon with a basket of Banbury and other cakes. (The Pantheon stands on Oxford Street, originally designed for concerts, it is only used for masquerades in the winter season.)

SIX BUNCHES A PENNY, SWEET LAVENDER!—A considerable quantity is sold to the middling-classes of the inhabitants, who are fond of placing lavender among their linen—the scent of which conquers that of the soap used in washing. (Temple Bar was erected to divide the strand from Fleet Street after the Great Fire and on the top were exhibited the heads of victims to the justice for the crime of high treason.)

SLIPPERS—The Turk is a portrait. He has sold Morocco Slippers in the Strand, Cheapside and Cornhill, a great number of years. There are other sellers, particularly about the Royal Exchange who are very importunate for custom while the venerable Turk uses no solicitation beyond showing his slippers. (Somerset House is a noble structure built by the government for the offices of public business.)

CHAPTER SIX

LUKE CLENNELL'S
LONDON MELODIES

THE HAWKERS in Luke Clennell's woodcuts look filthy, with bad skin and teeth, dressed in ragged clothes, either skinny as cadavers or fat as thieves, and with hands as scrawny as rats' claws. You can almost smell their bad breath and sweaty unwashed bodies, pushing themselves up against you in the crowd to make a hard sell.

Luke Clennell was apprenticed as an engraver to Thomas Bewick and then moved to London in 1804 as a young man, seeking a career as a painter and winning a major commission in 1816 from the Earl of Bridgewater to do portraits of more than four hundred guests at dinner in the Guildhall. The impossibility of getting all these subjects to sit for him drove Clennell to a nervous breakdown and he was committed to Salisbury Asylum. Although he recovered sufficiently to continue his career, he was afflicted with mental illness for the rest of his life and died in Newcastle Asylum in 1840.

The distinctive quality of Clennell's Cries, published as *London Melodies & Cries of the Seasons* in 1812, stands out among the hundreds of anonymous woodcuts published in chapbooks in the early nineteenth century by virtue of their lively texture and unapologetic, unsentimental portraiture.

Clennell's hawkers are never going to be framed on the parlour wall and they do not give a toss. They own their defiant, uncouth spirit. They are a rough bunch with ready fists that you would not wish to encounter in a narrow byway on a dark night. Yet they are survivors who know the lore of the streets, how to scratch a living out of little more than resourcefulness, and how to turn a shilling as easily as a groat.

With unrivalled spirit, savage humour, profane vocabulary and a rapacious appetite, Luke Clennell's woodcuts are the most street-wise of the Cries. He gloried in the grotesque features and unrestrained personalities of hawkers, while also permitting them an unbridled humanity that we can only regard with esteem.

Hot Mutton Dumplings—Nice Dumplings,
all Hot.

*Mackerel, O! Four for a Shilling,
Mackerel, O!*

Great News! Glorious News for Old England! Extraordinary Gazette.

*Come buy my Water Cresses, my nice young
Water Cresses.*

*Hastings, green and young Hastings! Here's
young Peas, Ten-pence a Peck, Marrow-
fat Peas.*

Buy a Mop, Brush, or a Hair Broom.

*Buy my Matches, good Lady.—Any good
Matches to day Ma'am.*

*Buy my Baskets, a Work, Fruit, or a
Bread Basket.*

*Chickens, a nice fat Chicken—Chicken, or a
young Fowl.*

*Ripe Asparagus, Three Shillings a Hundred.
Buy a Bundle, good and cheap.*

*Lilies of the Valley, sweet Lilies of the
Valley.*

*The King's Speech, the King's Speech to both
Houses of Parliament.*

*All round and sound, full weight, Three-
pence a Pound, my Ripe Kentish Cherries. Three-pence a Pound, Cherries.*

Buy my Oranges, nice China Oranges—
Rare sweet China.

Forty-a-Penny, young Radishes—Two score
a-Penny, Spring Radishes.

Buy my Herrings, fresh Herrings, O !
Three a Groat, Herrings O !

Buy a nice Wax Doll—rosy and fresh.

Sweep ! Sweep !—Sweep Soot, O !

Rabbit, Rabbit—Nice fat Rabbit.

CHAPTER SEVEN

JOHN THOMAS SMITH'S
VAGABONDIANA

ONE CAN ONLY WONDER if the unlikely location of John Thomas Smith's birth, in a Hackney carriage in Great Portland Street in 1766, granted him some special affinity with inhabitants of the London streets since his portraits of the urban dispossessed are some of the most humane. From the moment I cast my eyes upon his drawings, I was captivated by their vivid presence. As an engraver, Smith was able to translate his sketches directly into prints himself, conveying his distinctive vision without the mediation of others. There are few smiling faces because Smith allowed his subjects to retain their self-possession, but his acute calligraphic lines trace the intricate human detail of characters formed by their own ingenious survival strategies.

John Thomas Smith first published prints of the *Antiquities* and *Antient Topography of London*—those fragments of the city that had survived from before the Great Fire but which were vanishing in his time. Commonly, he populated these street views with Criers. They entered his vision as he sat in the street to draw ancient buildings and, recognising that they were integral to the urban landscape, it became the natural outcome of this work to focus upon portraits of these people.

In the opening pages of *Vagabondiana or Anecdotes of Mendicant Wanderers through the streets of London* published in 1816, Smith introduces his project to the reader with uneasy irony. 'Beggary, of late, has become so dreadful in London, that the more active interference of the legislature was deemed absolutely necessary, indeed the deceptions of the idle and sturdy were so various, cunning and extensive, that it was in most instances extremely difficult to discover the real

object of charity. Concluding, therefore, that from the reduction of metropolitan beggars, several curious characters would disappear by being either compelled to industry, or to partake of the liberal parochial rates, provided for them in their respective work-houses, it occurred to the author of the present publication, that likenesses of the most remarkable of them, with a few particulars of their habits, would not be unamusing to those to whom they have been a pest for several years.'

In spite of these moralistic tones, John Thomas Smith's pictures tell another story. The quality of his portraits transcend any condescension because, drawn by a sympathetic curiosity, he portrayed his vagabonds with dignity and wit. Smith represented them as one who walked the city his whole life, who knew his subjects personally, who drew them in the street and who narrowly escaped a lynch mob when he was once mistaken for a police sketch artist.

In a memoir of Smith, J. B. Nichols, his publisher, concluded, 'Mr Smith happily escaped the necessity of continuing his labours as an artist, being appointed keeper of prints & drawings at the British Museum.'

Smith described his subjects as 'curious characters' and while some may be exotic, it is obvious that these people cannot all fairly be classed as vagabonds, unless we choose instead to celebrate 'Vagabondiana' as the self-respecting state of those who an eek existence at the margins through their own wits.

Through pathos, John Thomas Smith sought to expose common human qualities and revealed his vagabonds as people rather than merely as pests to be driven out.

Pickled Cucumbers.

JOSEPH JOHNSON.

JEWISH MENDICANT.

GEORGE SMITH.

BILARDO MILLANO.

If I had as much money as I could tell,
I never would cry young lambs to sell !

ANATONY ANTONINI.

Staffordshire Ware Vendor.

Charles McGee.

William Conway, Spoon Seller.

Israel Potter, Chair Mender.

Buy a Mat.

Very Fine, Very Cheap.

JAMES SHARPE, THE FLYING PIE MAN.

NOTES ON SEVERAL PLATES

JOSEPH JOHNSON'S wounds rendered him incapable of further duty on the ocean and he was obliged to gain a living onshore. Novelty induced Joe to build a model of the ship *Nelson* to which, when placed on his cap, he could—by way of a bow of thanks or a supplicating inclination to a drawing room window—give the appearance of sea motion.

This JEWISH MENDICANT lost the use of his legs and was placed in a wooden cart so that he might be drawn about the neighbourhood of Petticoat Lane. His venerable appearance rendered it impossible for a Christian or a Jew to pass without giving alms, though he never begged but of his own people.

GEORGE SMITH was a brush maker who gave up his work due to rheumatism and took to selling groundsel and chickweed which he could obtain for free. Such was the popularity of singing birds, he was certain of a customer in every street and found he had no need to cry his chickweed, only to stand where the birds could see it.

BILARDO MILLANO, the bladder man, entertained crowds by playing upon his instrument contrived of strings that passed over a bladder and were drawn up to either end of a long stick, which instrument is said to have been the original hurdy-gurdy.

ANATONY ANTONINI was a native of Lucca in Tuscany, shown with his showboard of artificial flowers made of silk and paper, mounted upon wire stems and embellished with gaily-painted birds cast in wax.

THE itinerant STAFFORDSHIRE WARE VENDOR obtained his stock from Paddington basin where it was brought by water from the potteries and he travelled all over town to dispose of it at so moderate a rate that he could undersell the regular shopkeeper.

He was sure to sell something in every street since, in large households where the dustbin seldom passed a day without receiving the accidents to which the scullery was liable, they set aside at least ten pounds a year for replacements.

CHARLES McGEE was a native of Ribon, Jamaica, who was born in 1744 and whose father died at the age of one hundred and eight. He usually stood at the obelisk at the foot of Ludgate Hill. He had lost an eye and his woolly hair which was almost white was tied up behind in a tail with a large tuft at the end.

WILLIAM CONWAY, SPOON SELLER of Columbia Road, Bethnal Green. Born in 1752 in Worship Street, Norton Folgate, he followed his father as an itinerant trader forty-seven years earlier, walking twenty-five miles a day, six days a week and never knowing a day's illness. His shoes were made of the upper leather of old boots and lasted him six weeks.

ISRAEL POTTER, whom Smith described as, 'one of the oldest menders of chairs now living.' He rose at eight to cry through the streets yet Smith alleged that 'from the matted mass of dirty rushes thrown across his shoulders for months together, without ever being once opened, it must be concluded his cry of 'Old chairs to mend !' avails him but little—the fact is he goes his rounds and procures subsistence thus early in the morning for his daily wants.'

JAMES SHARPE, THE FLYING PIE MAN, sold his pies, walking about hatless, with his hair powdered, his dress neat, his apron spotless, jesting with a mighty voice in recommendation of puddings and pies, which he carried on a wooden platter. He was remarkable for his activity in disposing of goods by never standing still for a moment and crying 'All Hot, Red Hot!'

CHAPTER EIGHT

JEMMY CATNACH'S CRIES OF LONDON

POET, COMPOSITOR AND PUBLISHER, Jemmy (James) Catnach moved to London from Newcastle in 1812 and set up Seven Dials Press in Monmouth Court, producing more than four thousand chapbooks and broadsides in the next quarter century. Anointed as the high priest of street literature and eager to feed a seemingly-endless appetite for cheap printed novelties in the capital, Catnach put forth a multifarious list of titles, from lurid crime and political satire to juvenile rhymes and comic ballads, priced famously at a halfpenny or a 'farden.'

Unscrupulous in his pursuit of sales, in 1818 Catnach got caught out playing fast and loose with the truth when he published a bestselling pamphlet claiming that butchers in Drury Lane were passing off human flesh as pork in sausages, and he ended up in the House of Correction in Clerkenwell for six months. Such was Catnach's enthusiasm for ballads, Seven Dials Press kept a fiddler on the premises so singers could come in and audition their compositions for publication.

Of all the Cries in this book, these anonymous woodcuts are the most modestly-produced and crudely-wrought, yet I include them here as representative examples of the strong images and graphic vitality of the innumerable chapbooks produced on this subject in the eighteenth and nineteenth centuries. Such was the familiarity of representations of Cries that they became instantly recognisable even when reduced to folk icons.

Cherries.

Oranges.

Milk below.

Crumpling Codlings.

Filberts.

Clothes Pegs, Props, or Lines.

Sweep.

Peas & Beans.

Young Lambs to Sell.

Toys for Girls & Boys.

Strawberries.

All Hot Buns.

CHAPTER NINE

GEORGE SCHARF'S SKETCHBOOKS

GEORGE SCHARF'S arrival in London from Bavaria in 1816 coincided with the dawn of public advertising which saw every blank wall or hoarding plastered with posters, and people walking the streets carrying placards mounted on poles or sandwich boards. Over more than thirty years, Scharf applied his fluent draughtsmanship to recording every detail of London street life in his sketchbooks, delighting in the workaday life of the city, and produced for his personal satisfaction.

Although he had ambitions as a serious painter, Scharf never sold a picture but turned his talent instead to earning a living by producing medical, geological, zoological, topographical and architectural illustrations. His only popular success was a lithograph of London's first giraffes in 1836 that sold five hundred copies in two weeks.

Commissioned to record the construction of John Rennie's London Bridge in 1830, Scharf also documented the maze of streets that were lost in the creation of Trafalgar Square and it is his intricately observed drawings of the buildings, the shops and the people going about their ordinary business which are his unique legacy, communicating the drama of the city with unrivalled clarity and animation before the advent of photography.

Ladies embroidry frames

Cloths horses

Some of these first sketched in the Streets of
and afterwards copied on this paper at home

g. Scharf del
between 1830 & 40

fastnings of the Cloth horse

Shoes made
of carpet
of different
colours

hot pyes

don,
broom
made of
lit Cane

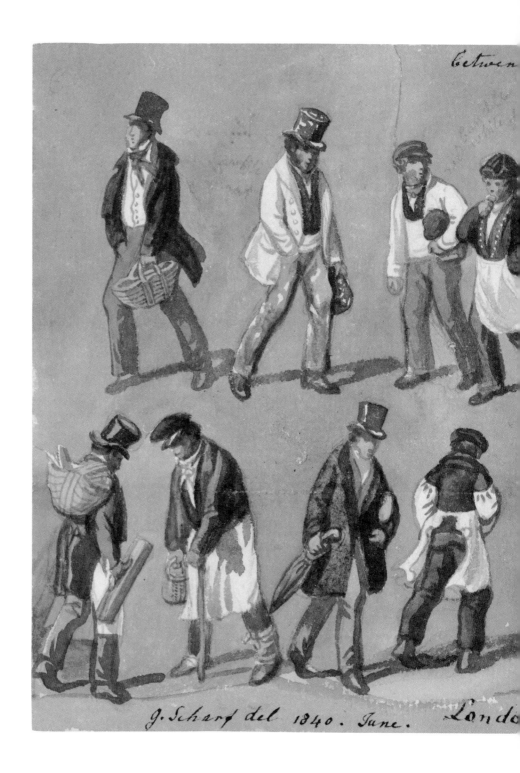

nd 6 O'Clock in the morn.g. in London Sumer

CHAPTER TEN
HENRY MAYHEW'S
LONDON LABOUR & LONDON POOR

IN THE PREFACE to *London Labour & London Poor*, Henry Mayhew described his work as 'the first attempt to publish the history of the people, from the lips of the people themselves—giving a literal description of their labour, their earnings, their trials and their sufferings in their own unvarnished language.' His interviews and pen portraits first appeared in the London Chronicle and were then collected in two volumes in 1851, before reaching their final form in five volumes as *London Labour & London Poor* published in 1865.

Mayhew's intention was to create a documentary record, educating his middle class readers about the lives of the poor to encourage social change. Yet his work transcends the politics of want and deprivation that he set out to address, because by telling their stories his subjects command our attention and win our respect. Henry Mayhew bears witness not only to the suffering of outcasts in nineteenth century London, but also to the resourcefulness and courage demonstrated by those who found ways of carving out lives in such unpromising circumstances.

Richard Beard took a set of daguerrotypes of Mayhew's subjects to accompany the interviews, but it was not possible to publish these directly in *London Labour & London Poor* and they were reproduced by engraving instead. Fortunately, since Beard's prints have not survived, the engravings were skillfully done.

In retrospect, these are especially fascinating images because they are the bridge between the tradition of artists' prints of Cries of London and the development of street photography, properly initiated ten years later by John Thomson's *Street Life in London*— the first book of photographs of street people in the capital.

When Richard Beard set out to photograph his subjects for Mayhew, the only representations he knew of street traders were those of the Cries and it is unsurprising that, compositionally and in the demeanour of the subjects, his photographs conform to this tradition. Only if you know their origin do you notice the effects of light and spontaneous detail in these images which are distinctive to photography.

TWO UNDER FIFTY FOR A FARDY'!

LONG-SONG SELLER.

THE LUCIFER MATCH GIRL.

THE ONE-LEGGED SWEEPER AT CHANCERY LANE.

THE STREET DOG-SELLER.

THE STREET-SELLER OF CROCKERY-WARE
BARTERING FOR OLD CLOTHES.

Dust Hoi ! Dust Hoi !

THE LONDON DUSTMAN.

THE CRIPPLED STREET BIRD-SELLER.

THE IRISH STREET-SELLER.

ONE OF THE FEW REMAINING
CLIMBING SWEEPS.

THE STREET-SELLER OF WALKING STICKS.

HINDU TRACT-SELLER.

JACK BLACK, HER MAJESTY'S RATCATCHER.

DOCTOR BOKANKY, THE STREET HERBALIST.

THE COSTER BOY AND GIRL
TOSSING THE PIEMAN.

THE STREET RHUBARB AND SPICE SELLER.

STREET-SELLER OF BIRDS' NESTS.

Notes on several plates

The One-Legged Crossing Sweeper—'I did not like the idea of being a crossing sweeper at first, till I reasoned with myself, 'Why should I mind? I'm not doing any hurt to any body.' I've been knocked down twice, sir—both times by cabs. The tradespeople never give me anything—not even a piece of bread.'

The Street-Seller of Dogs—'There's one advantage in my trade, we always has to do with the principals. I've known gentleman buy dogs for their misses. I might be sent on with them and if it was a two guinea dog or so, I was told never to give a hint of the price. It's easy for a gentleman that wants to please a lady, and not to lay out any great matter of tin, to say that what had really cost him two guineas, cost him twenty.'

The Crockery & Glass Wares Street-Seller—'A good tea service we generally give for a left-off suit of clothes, hat and boots. We give a sugar basin for an old coat and a rummer for a pair of old Wellington boots. For a glass milk jug, I should expect a waistcoat and trowsers, and they must be tidy ones too. If I go out with a fifteen shilling basket of crockery, maybe after a tidy day's work I shall come home with a shilling in my pocket and a bundle of old clothes, consisting of two or three old shirts, a coat or two, a suit of left-off livery, a woman's gown maybe or a pair of old stays, a couple of pairs of Wellingtons, and waistcoat or so.'

The Crippled Street Bird Seller—'I've been selling birds in the streets for six and twenty years. Father didn't know what better he could put me to, as I hadn't the right use of my hands or feet, and at first I did it very well. I liked the birds and I do still. I used to think they was like me, they was prisoners. At first I sold birds in Poplar, Limehouse and Blackwall. I've sold larks, linnets and goldfinches to captains of ships to take to the West Indies. They bring foreign birds here and take back London birds.'

Jack Black, Her Majesty's Rat Catcher—'The first rats I caught was when I was about nine years of age. I wasn't afraid to handle rats even then, it seemed to come natural to me. I've been bitten nearly everywhere, even where I can't name to you. I've got cages of iron wire, which I made myself, which will hold a thousand rats at a time, and I've had these cages of rats piled up with rats, solid like. Rats are everywhere about London, both rich and poor places'

Coster Boy & Girl Tossing the Pieman—If the pieman won the toss, he received a penny without giving a pie, if he lost he handed it over for nothing. 'Very few people buy without tossing, and boys in particular. Gentlemen out on the spree will frequently toss when they don't want the pies, and when they win they will amuse themselves by throwing the pies at one another, or at me. Sometimes I have taken as much as half a crown and the people of whom I had the money has never eaten a pie.'

The Street Rhubarb & Spice Seller—'I left my countree when I was sixteen or eighteen years of age, I forget. The people were Mahomedans in Mogadore, but we were Jews, just like here, you see. In my countree the governemen treat de Jews very badly, take all deir money. When I was a little shild, I hear talk of de people of my country sell de rhubarb in de streets of London, and make plenty money by it. Now dey all gone dead, and dere only four of us now in England. Two of us live in Mary Axe, anoder live in, what dey call dat—Spitalfield, and de oder in Petticoat Lane. De one wat live in Spitalfield is an old man, I dare say going on for seventy, and I am little better than seventy-three.'

The Street Seller of Birds' Nests—'I am a seller of birds'-nesties, snakes, slow-worms, adders, lizards, hedgehogs, frogs, and snails—that's all I sell in the summertime. I go out bird nesting three times a week. I start between one or two in the morning and walk all night. Oftentimes, I wouldn't take 'em if it wasn't for the want of the victuals, it seems such a pity to disturb 'em after they made their little bits of places.'

CHAPTER ELEVEN

JOHN THOMSON'S
STREET LIFE IN LONDON

PHOTOGRAPHER JOHN THOMSON began publishing his monthly magazine *Street Life in London* in 1876, presenting his photographs accompanied with pen portraits by Adolphe Smith.

It was the first attempt to use photojournalism to record the lives of Londoners but, in his photography, Thomson adopted compositions and content that were familiar archetypes in the Cries tradition—the chair mender, the sweep and the strawberry seller. Yet although Thomson composed his photographs to create picturesque images, in many cases the subjects themselves succeed in taking possession of the pictures, aided by Adolphe Smith's texts underlining the harsh social realities of their existence.

Even if they did not acknowledge or even recognise it, John Thomson's subjects had an element of choice in how they presented themselves to the camera and the resulting image became a collaboration between the photographer and the subject. Previously, artists had complete control of how they chose to represent Criers but photography changed this relationship,

granting subjects the opportunity to assert themselves before the lens.

When I look at John Thomson's photographs, I am startled by the power of the gaze of those who look straight at the camera and connect with us directly, while there is a plangent sadness to those with eyes cast down in subservience. Seen in the light of Adolphe Smith's pen portraits outlining their circumstances, John Thomson's subjects become monumental in their dignified stillness—as if their phlegmatic attitudes manifest a strength of character and stoicism in the face of a life of hard work.

The photograph can record an instant of frozen enactment, like the bill stickers demonstrating what they do for the camera, but more interesting are the equivocal moments where there is human exposure. In each of these pictures, there is an unresolved tension—even as the camera records a moment of hiatus, we know it is an interruption before the drama resumes.

The London Boardmen.

BILL STICKERS.

THE TEMPERANCE SWEEP.

Street Doctor.

CANEY THE CLOWN.

Notes on the plates

Excerpts from descriptions accompanying the plates by Adophe Smith

THE LONDON BOARDMEN—'Boardmen are recruited among the most hopeless of our poor. Often men who have fallen in the world, some have even once enjoyed the title of 'gentlemen,' boast of an excellent education, but have been reduced to their present pitch of degradation by what they fashionably term 'dipsomania'! If they walk on the pavement, the police indignantly throw them off into the gutter, where they become entangled in the wheels of carriages, and where cabs and omnibuses are ruthlessly driven against them.'

BILL STICKERS—'As a rule, once a man has become proficient in the art of bill-pasting, he rarely abandons this style of work. This is due to fact that many of them have never done anything else and were, as my informant put it, 'born in a paste can.' There is a certain knack required in pasting a bill on a rough board, but the difficulty is increased fourfold when it is necessary to climb a high ladder, paste can, bills and brush in hand. The wind will probably blow the advertisement to pieces before it can be affixed to the wall unless the bill sticker is cool, prompt in his actions and steady of foot.'

THE TEMPERANCE SWEEP—'To his newly acquired sobriety, monetary prosperity soon ensued and he is well known throughout the neighbourhood, where he advocates the cause of total abstinence ...'

STREET DOCTOR—'Vendors of pills, potions and quack nostrums are not quite so numerous as they were in former days. The increasing number of free hospitals where the poor may consult qualified physicians have tended to sweep this class of street folks from the thoroughfares of London.'

CANEY THE CLOWN—'Thousands remember how he delighted them with his string of sausages at the yearly pantomime, but Caney has cut his last caper since his exertions to please at Stepney Fair caused the bursting of a varicose vein in his leg and, although his careworn face fails to reflect his natural joviality, the mending of chairs brings him constant employment.'

CHAPTER TWELVE

JOHN PLAYER'S CRIES OF LONDON

JOHN PLAYER & SONS put collectors' cards in their cigarette packets from 1893 and it is a measure of the popularity of the Cries of London series, issued at first in 1912 in two sets of large-format cards, that they were expanded subsequently into two further series of twenty-five smaller cards. These gaudy prints of cheerful hawkers in colourful dress were highly collectable, even if historical veracity was sacrificed for the sake of popular appeal.

Cries by Marcellus Laroon, William Marshall Craig and John Thomas Smith were reworked by anonymous commercial artists in the style of Francis Wheatley to create a lively gallery of hawkers from all historical periods crowding the thoroughfares of a mythic city. Old London became transformed into an ahistorical metropolis of swashbuckling romance in these cards, where the streets were as bright as pantomime backdrops and the traders swaggered like music hall acts, ready to burst into song.

Yet, thumbing through these modest little cards with their corners rounded from use, no-one can deny the affectionate quality of these images and the fond significance that collectors gave to these ephemera, investing them with an emotional meaning which transcends the sentimental whimsy of the images, the quaint self-conscious archaic spellings, the curious anecdotal texts, the grubbiness and the crude printing. Collectors recognised that the Cries of London celebrated the ingenuity and stamina of those with nothing who for centuries eeked out a living upon the streets of London by hawking, and used their wits to do it with panache, transforming commerce into culture in the process.

In this most-popular incarnation as cigarette cards, the Cries of London were celebrating a history of poverty retold as the brave and self-respecting history of resourcefulness. Once collected by schoolchildren in class and soldiers in the trenches as minor tokens of intangible value, they passed through so many hands before they arrived in mine. In the process, they became transformed into beloved totems of the collective history of Londoners.

CRIES OF LONDON

9

Hair Brooms.

In Shakespeare's time the Broom Men (in common with the fish-wives and the costard-mongers) were notorious for the loudness of their cries. A considerable trade was done in those days by bartering, the broom-seller being willing to exchange "*New Brooms for Old Shoes.*" The more respectable class of traders sold, in addition to brooms, sieves, bowls, clothes-horses, and many other articles of domestic utility.

ISSUED BY
John Player & Sons.
BRANCH OF THE IMPERIAL TOBACCO CO (OF GREAT BRITAIN & IRELAND), LTD.

CRIES OF LONDON

11

Dust, Ho!

In the days before Municipal Sanitary Authorities arranged for the disposal of ashes and dust, private individuals sent round their carts to collect this refuse which was carried to the yards, where it was afterwards sifted and disposed of for various purposes. The dust-carts plied through the streets every morning, attended by men ringing large bells and calling "*Dust, Ho! Dust, Ho! Bring out your dust.*"

ISSUED BY
John Player & Sons.
BRANCH OF THE IMPERIAL TOBACCO CO (OF GREAT BRITAIN & IRELAND), LTD.

CRIES OF LONDON

16

Turnips and Carrots Ho.

The cry of the Vegetable Seller has undergone many variations since the traders of the 17th century cried "*Buy any Turneps!*" and "*Whyt Carots, whyt!*" In more recent years the cry was "*Two pence a bunch, young Carrots, ho!*" The costermongers, male and female, plied their trade in Shakespeare's day, when they were known as *costard-mongers*, or *apple-sellers*. Even at that date the loudness of their cries was proverbial.

ISSUED BY
John Player & Sons.
BRANCH OF THE IMPERIAL TOBACCO CO (OF GREAT BRITAIN & IRELAND), LTD.

CRIES OF LONDON

12

Sweep Soot, Ho!

The Chimney Sweeping industry has been extensively reformed during the last hundred years. The sweep of the 18th century gathered his apprentices from the parish workhouses, and usually selected the smallest of them, who were the better able to ascend and sweep the chimneys. An Act of Parliament compelled every sweep's apprentice to wear in front of his cap a brass plate engraved with his master's name.

ISSUED BY
John Player & Sons.
BRANCH OF THE IMPERIAL TOBACCO CO (OF GREAT BRITAIN & IRELAND), LTD.

CRIES OF LONDON

8

Cats' and Dogs' Meat!

The unsavoury occupation of dealer in cats' meat appears to have been followed almost exclusively by women, who retailed their goods by weight. Cruikshank has depicted one of these surrounded by her retinue of cats of all kinds; while beneath is the quaint verse—
"*Here's famous meat—all lean, no fat—
No better in Great Britain;
Come, buy a penn'orth for your Cat—
A happ'orth for your Kitten.*"

ISSUED BY
John Player & Sons.
BRANCH OF THE IMPERIAL TOBACCO CO (OF GREAT BRITAIN & IRELAND), LTD.

CRIES OF LONDON

19

Maids, Buy a Mop.

"*Buy a Mop! Buy a Broom! Good to-day!*" Although the lady shown in our picture seems to have specialised in mops, it was not unusual for the street trader to carry, in addition to mops and brushes of all kinds, clothes-horses, lines, and various hardware goods. An 18th century woodcut shows the dealer in Mops plying her trade, with the rhyming invitation—
"*Ye cleanly housewives come to me,
And buy a Mop or Broom,
To sweep your chambers,
scour your stairs,
Or wash your sitting room.*"

ISSUED BY
John Player & Sons.
BRANCH OF THE IMPERIAL TOBACCO CO (OF GREAT BRITAIN & IRELAND), LTD.

CRIES OF LONDON

14

Strawberrys Scarlet Strawberrys.

During the height of the strawberry season the vendors of strawberries, both men and women, cried their wares through the streets and suburbs of London. The freshly-gathered fruit was sold in "potties," or long baskets of plaited wood, each containing about a quart of strawberries. One penny was charged for the "pottle," the money being remitted if the basket was returned. Strawberries appear to have been sold in London as early as 1400.

ISSUED BY
John Player & Sons.
BRANCH OF THE IMPERIAL TOBACCO CO (OF GREAT BRITAIN & IRELAND), LTD.

CRIES OF LONDON

7

Buy a Fine Singing Bird.

The seller of birds, with his cages of feathered songsters and his cry of "*Come buy my singing birds,*" or "*Buy a linnet or a goldfinch,*" has long disappeared from our city streets. In the reign of Charles II., the keeping of caged birds was very much more popular than it is to-day. At that time the Birdcage Walk, on the south side of St. James's Park, was lined with aviaries of singing birds belonging to the "merry monarch."

ISSUED BY
John Player & Sons.
BRANCH OF THE IMPERIAL TOBACCO CO (OF GREAT BRITAIN & IRELAND), LTD.

CRIES OF LONDON

13

Cowcumbers to Pickle.

The seller of cucumbers seems to have varied his cries somewhat. In the days of Elizabeth he cried "*Buy any cucumber,*" and sixty years later we have "*I ha' ripe cowcumber, ripe cowcumber.*" An 18th century engraving of a woman selling cucumbers bears the title, "*Delicate cowcumbers to pickle,*" and a woodcut of rather later date invites us to "*Buy green and large cucumbers, green and large cucumbers, twelve a penny.*"

ISSUED BY
John Player & Sons.
BRANCH OF THE IMPERIAL TOBACCO CO (OF GREAT BRITAIN & IRELAND), LTD.

CRIES OF LONDON

14

Ripe Asparagus.

Asparagus has for centuries been sold in the thoroughfares of London to the accompaniment of such odd cries as "*Ripe speregas,*" and "*Ripe sparrowgrass.*" One of the best known of the Roxburghe Ballads, now in the British Museum, and dating probably from the 17th century, records the cry as, "*Here's collyflowers and asparagus.*" Not only vegetables, but such herbs as fatherfew, gilliflowers, rue, balm, hissop, scurvy-grass, &c., were sold in the streets.

ISSUED BY
John Player & Sons.
BRANCH OF THE IMPERIAL TOBACCO CO (OF GREAT BRITAIN & IRELAND), LTD.

CRIES OF LONDON

11

Any Work for John Cooper.

Many of the working trades have long since disappeared from our thoroughfares, and although the menders of chairs and the travelling knife-grinder are still with us, the travelling cooper has vanished. His cry, "*Any work for John Cooper,*" recalls a time when wooden tubs and pails were more generally used in households than they are to-day. The familiar surname of Cooper is, of course, of trade origin.

ISSUED BY
John Player & Sons.
BRANCH OF THE IMPERIAL TOBACCO CO (OF GREAT BRITAIN & IRELAND), LTD.

CRIES OF LONDON

17

Diddle, Diddle, Diddle, Dumplens, ho!

Many street traders indulged in a sort of singing refrain such as that of the seller of dumplings; "*Diddle, diddle dumplins, ho!*" and the "*Ti-tid-ty-tiddy-loll.*" Here is your nice gingerbread" of the vendor of gingerbread-cake. Traders in pies and dumplings used to call at the taverns to find customers, with whom they frequently settled the price of their wares by playing "pitch and toss."

ISSUED BY
John Player & Sons.
BRANCH OF THE IMPERIAL TOBACCO CO (OF GREAT BRITAIN & IRELAND), LTD.

PLAYER'S CIGARETTES.

HAIR BROOMS.

PLAYER'S CIGARETTES

DUST HO!

PLAYER'S CIGARETTES

TURNIPS & CARROTS HO.

PLAYER'S CIGARETTES

SWEEP SOOT HO!

PLAYER'S CIGARETTES.

CAT'S & DOG'S MEAT!

PLAYER'S CIGARETTES

MAIDS, BUY A MOP.

PLAYER'S CIGARETTES

STRAWBERRYS SCARLET STRAWBERRYS

PLAYER'S CIGARETTES

BUY A FINE SINGING BIRD

PLAYER'S CIGARETTES.

COWCUMBERS TO PICKLE

PLAYER'S CIGARETTES.

RIPE ASPARAGUS.

PLAYER'S CIGARETTES

ANY WORK FOR IOHN COOPER

PLAYER'S CIGARETTES.

DIDDLE DIDDLE DIDDLE
DUMPLENS HO!

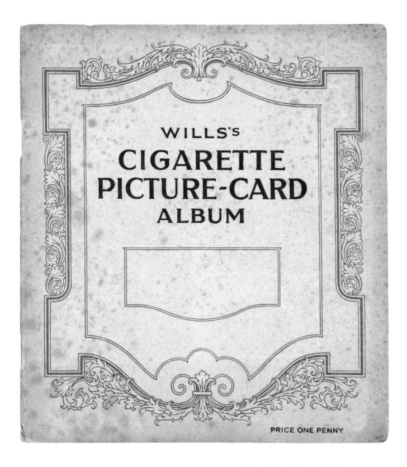

*Complete sets of cigarette cards were collected and cherished
in cardboard albums such as this one*

Chapter Thirteen

JULIUS MENDES PRICE'S TYPES OF LONDON

WAR ARTIST Julius Mendes Price wrote and illustrated this series of eighty cards distributed by Black Cat Cigarettes from 1919. Born in St Pancras in 1857, Price pursued the subject of war both as an artist and as a correspondent through a sequence of conflicts between 1884 and 1916.

His *Types of London* serve as a sober counterpoint to John Player's *Cries of London*, by introducing a contemporary realism in the selection and portrayal of Londoners.

John Thomas Smith and William Craig Marshall had included wounded veterans on the street a century earlier, but Price illustrated an entire society living in the shadow of war, featuring servicemen and women of different ranks and forces, and including a military nurse and a recruiting sergeant.

Age-old figures such the cats' meat man, the muffin man and the chairmender appear in their familiar guises alongside new arrivals to the scene like the attendant at the cheap picture theatre, the telephone girl and the female window cleaner. In Price's *London Types*, the lavender seller, which traditionally offered the opportunity of a romantic pastoral image, is represented by a shabby downtrodden man with a cardboard tray of lavender bags.

In Julius Mendes Price's unsentimental vision of London at the end of the First World War, the lyricism of earlier Cries had been dispelled and traditional hawkers became anachronisms within a wider social panorama in which agents of social control featured prominently—such as the superintendent of the receiving ward for females at the workhouse, the Thames police officer, the police matron, the special constable and the police court jailer.

TYPES OF LONDON

A Series of Drawings by
JULIUS M. PRICE
War Artist and Correspondent

No. 15—Catsmeat Man

THE Catsmeat Man's advent is eagerly looked for by London's hungry pussies. With cool deliberation he affixes the unsavoury morsels upon wooden skewers, scarcely deigning the while to even glance at the expectant animals grouped about his barrow

Issued by
CARRERAS LIMITED
ESTAB. 1788
LONDON   MONTREAL
ENG.   QUE.

TYPES OF LONDON

A Series of Drawings by
JULIUS M. PRICE
War Artist and Correspondent

No. 50—"Sweet Lavender"

AMONG the cries of London none is more quaint and weird than that of "Blooming Lavender." It strikes a note of sadness, however—it is the harbinger of departing summer. Lavender is extensively cultivated in the neighbourhood of Mitcham; its fragrant odour, so beloved by our grandmothers.

Issued by
CARRERAS LIMITED
ESTAB. 1788
LONDON   MONTREAL
ENG.   QUE.

TYPES OF LONDON

A Series of Drawings by
JULIUS M. PRICE
War Artist and Correspondent

No. 2—Shoe-black

THE Shoe-black has for many years been a feature of London life and his red coat imparts a welcome touch of colour to the streets of the Metropolis. The Great War summons evoked an instantaneous response from London Shoe-blacks, and many acts of gallantry on land and sea have been credited to them.

Issued by
CARRERAS LIMITED
ESTAB. 1788
LONDON   MONTREAL
ENG.   QUE.

TYPES OF LONDON

A Series of Drawings by
JULIUS M. PRICE
War Artist and Correspondent

No. 47—Chair Mender

THE open-air Chair Mender is quite an unusual sight in London, although nowadays one is astonished at nothing. Like so many other old-fashioned trades, he is gradually being superseded by modern improvements.

Issued by
CARRERAS LIMITED
ESTAB. 1788
LONDON   MONTREAL
ENG.   QUE.

TYPES OF LONDON

A Series of Drawings by
JULIUS M. PRICE
War Artist and Correspondent

No. 33—Muffin-man

THE Muffin-man with his bell echoing through the deserted streets accentuates the gloom and dreariness of London on a wet Sunday afternoon in the late Autumn or Winter, and makes one appreciate the while to more the cosy fire, cheerful company and nice hot muffins for tea.

Issued by
CARRERAS LIMITED
ESTAB. 1788
LONDON   MONTREAL
ENG.   QUE.

TYPES OF LONDON

A Series of Drawings by
JULIUS M. PRICE
War Artist and Correspondent

No. 21—Recruiting Petty Officer in the Navy

PETTY OFFICERS who possess persuasive eloquence and alertness are appointed to recruit for the Navy. They accept only recruits of unblemished character and the result of this wise discrimination is evidenced by the splendid work of every branch of the British Navy of to-day.

Issued by
CARRERAS LIMITED
ESTAB. 1788
LONDON   MONTREAL
ENG.   QUE.

TYPES OF LONDON

A Series of Drawings by
JULIUS M. PRICE
War Artist and Correspondent

No. 11—Costermonger

THE London Costermonger's repartee and resourcefulness are known the world over. Fish, flesh, fowl, or vegetables—(nothing comes amiss to him) are dealt in with an impartiality that is deserving of larger profits and wider recognition.

Issued by
CARRERAS LIMITED
ESTAB. 1788
LONDON   MONTREAL
ENG.   QUE.

TYPES OF LONDON

A Series of Drawings by
JULIUS M. PRICE
War Artist and Correspondent

No. 44—Flower Girl

THE Flower Girl and her wares supply an artistic touch of colour to the prevailing dulness of the streets and squares of London. Her desire to please is only equalled by her industry and knowledge of flowers.

Issued by
CARRERAS LIMITED
ESTAB. 1788
LONDON   MONTREAL
ENG.   QUE.

TYPES OF LONDON

A Series of Drawings by
JULIUS M. PRICE
War Artist and Correspondent

No. 22—Sweep

AN arduous, unpleasant, but necessary labour is the lot of London's Chimney Sweeps. With the extensive use of gas fires the days of the sweep, however, are gradually passing away and it is hoped that at no distant date we shall be well on the way to a smokeless London.

Issued by
CARRERAS LIMITED
ESTAB. 1788
LONDON   MONTREAL
ENG.   QUE.

TYPES OF LONDON

A Series of Drawings by
JULIUS M. PRICE
War Artist and Correspondent

No. 5—Newspaper Boy

WAR-TIME exigencies and paper shortage deprive the London newspaper boy of two familiar features. No longer must the air ring with his penetrating voice, while the contents bills with their startling headlines have been regretfully laid aside.

Issued by
CARRERAS LIMITED
ESTAB. 1788
LONDON   MONTREAL
ENG.   QUE.

TYPES OF LONDON

A Series of Drawings by
JULIUS M. PRICE
War Artist and Correspondent

No. 13—Street Musician

THE itinerant musician is a very common sight in all big cities though in many cases it is but a cloak for begging. Occasionally some slight semblance of melody may be discerned, but, as a general rule, it is to be wondered how the "musicians" can earn a livelihood, so discordant is their noise.

Issued by
CARRERAS LIMITED
ESTAB. 1788
LONDON   MONTREAL
ENG.   QUE.

TYPES OF LONDON

A Series of Drawings by
JULIUS M. PRICE
War Artist and Correspondent

No. 34—Sandwich-man

ALTHOUGH the occupation of a Sandwich-man offers no inducements to the ambitious, it is a more useful calling than at first sight appears. This method of advertising is often more successful than newspapers or journals in reaching certain sections of the public, and therefore must not be too slightingly regarded.

Issued by
CARRERAS LIMITED
ESTAB. 1788
LONDON   MONTREAL
ENG.   QUE.

BLACK CAT
CIGARETTES

CATSMEAT MAN

BLACK CAT
CIGARETTES

"SWEET LAVENDER"

BLACK CAT
CIGARETTES

SHOE-BLACK

BLACK CAT
CIGARETTES

CHAIR MENDER

BLACK CAT
CIGARETTES

MUFFIN MAN

BLACK CAT
CIGARETTES

RECRUITING PETTY OFFICER
IN THE NAVY

BLACK CAT
CIGARETTES

COSTERMONGER

BLACK CAT
CIGARETTES

FLOWER GIRL

BLACK CAT
CIGARETTES

SWEEP

BLACK CAT
CIGARETTES

NEWSPAPER BOY

BLACK CAT
CIGARETTES

STREET MUSICIAN

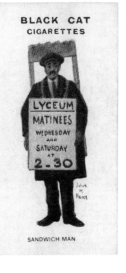

BLACK CAT
CIGARETTES

SANDWICH MAN

CHAPTER FOURTEEN

THE CURIOUS LEGACY OF FRANCIS WHEATLEY

ALTHOUGH HE RECEIVED little recognition in his lifetime, Francis Wheatley created the most famous images of Cries of London which are still universally recognised today. By accident of fate, his work achieved its greatest success in the early twentieth century, gaining widespread popularity and becoming symbolic of the romance of old London—until it fell out of favour with subsequent generations, devalued by its ubiquity and dismissed as sentimental cliche.

Yet once you know the circumstances of the creation of Francis Wheatley's *London Cries*, it is not so easy to write them off and they deserve better than being consigned to the dustbin of cultural history. His Cries became commonplace in the twentieth century because people loved them, investing personal meaning in these cheaply distributed images and, by treasuring these mass-produced souvenirs, trinkets and keepsakes, they charged them with genuine significance.

The catalyst for the revival came in 1913 when Yardley of London, cosmetic and soap manufacturers, adopted Wheatley's primrose seller as their symbol, replacing primroses with sheafs of lavender to illustrate their most popular fragrance, Old English Lavender.

Established in 1770, Yardley sought an image that reflected the era of their origin and the lavender grown for the company in the south east of England. By publishing Wheatley's image upon countless thousands of soap boxes and talcum powder tins, Yardley won such a popular success that it is still in use upon their packaging over a century later.

Player's cigarette cards included Wheatley's images in their set of Cries, 'after the Celebrated Pictures by F. Wheatley & others,' and, through the twentieth century, his Cries were reprinted endlessly in many guises and upon all kinds of souvenirs and knick-knacks as popular icons, representing the collective emotional ownership that Londoners felt for the ancient capital and its wonders.

Even today, if people do not know the name, it is unlikely they do not recognise Wheatley's work. They may have seen prints of his Cries being sold off cheaply at car boot sales and in charity shops, or reproduced upon talcum powder tins and soap boxes, or perhaps they have driven past his figures, twenty-feet-high on the side of the former Yardley factory in Stratford, East London.

LINEN AND COTTON   LAMONT reg 1071

CRIES of LONDON

Two bunches a penny primroses, two bunches a penny · A un sol mes deux poignées de primeroses, a unsol

Irish linen and cotton tea towel by Samuel Lamont & Sons, Armagh

Souvenir biscuit tins produced by Huntley & Palmers and Peek Freans

Silk scarf by Jacqmar of Mayfair

Variant plates by Adams of Burslem from the Cries of London dinner service produced between 1920 and 1965

CHAPTER FIFTEEN

TONY HAWKINS, RETIRED PEDLAR

Tony Hawkins

TONY HAWKINS testified to me that he sold peanuts and roasted chestnuts in the West End streets for ten years, but—after getting arrested and roughed up by the police eighty-seven times—his health failed and he retired.

Whereas Tony used to visit Gardners' Market Sundriesmen in Commercial Street, Spitalfields regularly to buy bags for his thriving business, after retirement he came simply to pass the time with his old friend Paul Gardner.

It was Paul who effected my introduction to Tony, a man with a defiant strength of character, frail physically yet energised by moral courage. Brandishing the dog-eared stack of paperwork from his eighty-seven court cases, he was immensely proud that he won every one and it was proven he never broke the law once.

Tony's pitiful catalogue of his wrangles with Westminster Council—who went to extreme lengths just to prevent him peddling nuts in Piccadilly—reveal that the age-old ambivalence and prejudice against those who seek to make a modest living by trading in the street persists to the present day.

'I was unemployed as a labourer in Manchester, so I started off as a pedlar. I sold socks, balloons—anything really. A pedlar trades as he travels, and the will to support myself and the bright lights brought me to London. I was peddling around the West End selling peanuts mostly but also chestnuts. I sold flags at football matches too, Chelsea and Arsenal.

'In the nineteen-eighties, a sergeant took me to Bow Street Magistrates Court for selling peanuts in Piccadilly. So I went along, it was no big deal. I admitted I was trading and I was a licenced pedlar.

'In Court, they were amazed because thay hadn't seen many pedlars, there were only half a dozen in the West End. I won the case and I went to shake the sergeant's hand afterwards, but he pushed me away and said it wasn't the end of it. He told me he'd do everything in his power to make sure I never worked again and he hounded me after that. He said, 'If you're going to do it again, we will arrest you again,' and I've been arrested more than eighty times and spent nights in cells. I've been roughed up so many times by policemen and council enforcement officers that I had to get a hidden camera because I feared for my safety.

'They confiscated my stock and equipment from me every time I was charged with the offence of street trading without a licence, when I had a Pedlar's Licence issued in accordance with the Pedlar's Act of 1871. The original Act was passed in the eighteenth century so that veteran soldiers could trade in fish, fruit, vegetables and victuals, and be distinguished from vagabonds. Anyone over the age of seventeen can get a pedlar's licence as long as you have no criminal record. According to the Bill of Rights and the Magna Carta, every person in this country has the right to trade.

'I went to the High Court once when they found against me and the judge overturned it in my favour. But then in 2000 they brought in the Westminster Act because of people like myself. Westminster Council juggled the words so that it states that pedlars are only allowed to go door-to-door.

'Prior to that Act, we were allowed to peddle lawfully anywhere in the United Kingdom but now the Act is also being used to stop pedlars in Newcastle, Liverpool, Manchester, Warrington and Balham. Yet Acts and Statutes are not laws, they are rules for the governance, accepted only by consent of the populace.

'Once, I went to get my stuff back from Westminster Council and I met the Manager of Licencing & Street Enforcement. I asked him, 'Why do you continue to waste the money of the council tax payers with so many cases against me when you haven't won a single one?'

'Your lawyer, Mr Barca, I'm sick of him,' he said, 'He only represents the lower end of the market like you, and pimps and prostitutes.' Later, he denied it and said he had a witness too, but I had recorded him and he had to pay four thousand pounds in damages to Mr Barca.

'After being hounded by the council and the police so many times, I've become narked and with good reason. Over the years, it has cost me a fortune to pay the legal costs. I had to work to earn all the money to pay for it. I regard myself as downtrodden because I was never allowed to benefit from my hard work, but if I had been allowed to continue trading, I could have owned a house by now and have some money in the bank.

'People say to me, 'Why have you done it?' I have done it because I believe in the right to trade freely as a human right.'

Tony is now retired, living comfortably in sheltered housing, and has become a self-taught yet highly articulate expert in the law regarding pedlars and street trading, and he is involved with the Pedlars Information & Resource Centre.

Despite losing his health and his livelihood, Tony has acquired moral stature, passionate to support others suffering similar harassment because they exercise their right to sell in the street. With exceptional perseverance, acting out of a love of liberty and a refusal to be intimidated by authority, Tony Hawkins is an unacknowledged hero of the London streets.

ACKNOWLEDGEMENTS

This book is published with the generous investment
of the following readers of *Spitalfields Life*:

Fiona Atkins, Dana Burstow, Peter Cameron, Tamara Cartwright-Loebl, Charlie De Wet, Keith Evans, John Gillman & Mary Winch, Mark Hamsher & Elna Jacobs, Hilda Kean, Michael Keating, Libby Hall, Stella Herbert, Colin Lennon, David Lewis, Julia Meadows, Richard Metcalfe, Carl Moss, Angus Murray, Tatiana Nye, Frances Oakley, Frank Reynolds, Corvin Roman, Tim Sayer, Elizabeth Scott, Aubrey Silkoff, Julian Woodford, Graham Williams, Jane Williamson & Erminia Yardley.

Although there have been few books on the subject of Cries of London, this current work could not exist without the inspiring precedents set by Charles Hindley and Andrew Tuer in the nineteenth century, and Sean Shesgreen in our own time.

I owe a debt of gratitude to Stefan Dickers, Archives & Library Manager at Bishopsgate Institute, who introduced me to the great variety of sets of Cries in the London Collection at the Institute over the last five years. The Cries drawn by Marcellus Laroon, Francis Wheatley and William Marshall Craig, those engraved by Luke Clennell and John Thomas Smith, those published by Jemmy Catnach and Henry Mayhew, and those photographed by John Thomson are all reproduced courtesy of Bishopsgate Institute.

Pepys Library at Magdalene College, Cambridge, supplied the anonymous sets of woodcuts and engravings of Cries from Samuel Pepys' London & Westminster Album. © Pepys Library, Magdalene College. All rights reserved.

Paul Mellon Centre for Studies in British Art, Yale University, supplied Paul Sandby's drawings and Museum of London supplied the engraved frontispiece to the printed edition of his Cries. © Museum of London. All rights reserved.

British Museum Department of Prints & Drawings supplied George Scharf's drawings. © The Trustees of the British Museum. All rights reserved.

John Player Cigarette Cards, Black Cat Cigarette Cards and Francis Wheatley memorabilia are from The Gentle Author's personal collection. Portrait of Tony Hawkins by The Gentle Author.

Thanks are due to the scholarship of Dr Ruth Richardson who identified Luke Clennell's *London Melodies* which were formerly published anonymously and are ascribed to their creator for the first time in this book.

Also published by Spitalfields Life Books

Travellers' Children in London Fields COLIN O'BRIEN

The Gentle Author's London Album

Brick Lane PHIL MAXWELL

Underground BOB MAZZER

Spitalfields Nippers HORACE WARNER

London Life COLIN O'BRIEN

Baddeley Brothers